Mulberry AT HOME

ROGER SAUL

Mulberry

AT HOME

EBURY PRESS
LONDON

First published in Great Britain in 1999

1 3 5 7 9 10 8 6 4 2

First published by Ebury Press,
Random House, 20 Vauxhall Bridge Road, London SW1V 2SA

Random House Australia (Pty) Limited,
20 Alfred Street, Milsons Point, Sydney, New South Wales 2061, Australia

Random House New Zealand Limited,
18 Poland Road, Glenfield, Auckland 10, New Zealand

Random House South Africa (Pty) Limited,
Endulini, 5a Jubilee Road, Parktown 2193, South Africa

The Random House Group Limited Reg. No. 954009

A CIP catalogue record for this book is available from the British Library.

Managing Director of Mulberry Home Jill Evans
International Mulberry Home PR & Project Executive Victoria Murray
Designer Debbie Mole
Photographer Bill Batten
Stylist Arabella McNie

ISBN 0 09 186812 2

Printed and bound in Hong Kong by C&C offset Printing Co., Ltd.

Papers used by Ebury Press are natural, recyclable products made from wood grown in sustainable forests.

Contents

REAL TASTE is as rare as some rainforest orchids. Anyone can buy a certain kind of taste in Bond Street or find it in numerous magazines, yet true, individual taste cannot simply be bought. If you possess this, together with the guts to be true to yourself, then you may succeed.

ROGER SAUL has this individual taste, making him stand out in a society which values conformity above magic and wisdom. His book allows us to share his talents and vision, enabling us to make our home environment a more exciting place to be.

David Bailey

Introduction

I AM OFTEN *asked why I started Mulberry Home. As we designed and opened more and more Mulberry shops around the world in the '80s, we were told with increasing frequency by our customers that they felt 'at home' in our shops — so much so that they often tried to buy our shop furnishings. Sometimes they even succeeded — I remember a lady in Tokyo insisting on buying our changing room curtains! It seemed a natural progression to develop our own 'Home Collection' in 1991, which was launched at Harvey Nichols in London by HRH the Princess Royal.*

At that time the Gulf War was on, and people had suddenly become more conscious of how precious home life was. They wanted instead a home environment that expressed their need for comfort, stability and security. Our 'Home Collection' fitted the bill.

Living as I do in the heart of a rural county of England, it would be impossible not to be influenced by the traditions and pursuits I am in touch with daily. Racing, hunting, shooting and fishing are still as popular in Somerset today as they were in Henry VIII's reign – around the time that the house that I now live in was originally built – but my interest in them has as much to do with the spirit and style in which they are conducted as in the nature of the pursuits themselves. From the gloriously coloured silks worn by jockeys to the irridescent colours of feathers or a pair of bespoke riding boots, I am won over by the sheer quality of colour, texture and form. It is just this perfect marriage of form and function that I aspire to create in the furnishings we design at Mulberry.

Architecture and travel are probably my greatest influences. In fabric design terms, we are lucky to have the freedom, in our imagination, to head off to all sorts of exotic places, although we try to keep ourselves to areas that have been influenced culturally and geographically by the British over the years. Architectural heritage is an area of endless fascination and, when toying with the design for a room or a garden, I've often found that the key can be to use something I have found to kick-start the concept, be it a pair of Indian columns, a theatre balcony or a plaster relief of cherubs, as you will see for yourselves on the pages that follow.

From an early age, I was fascinated by the glamour and panache of all things military. My father's old uniform saw active service again with the six-year-old Roger Saul. The Carnaby Street fad of wearing Sergeant Pepper-style Victorian military uniforms gave me the chance both to wear and collect some amazing outfits. It also took me to London's Portobello Road and my first trading activity. Throughout my career at Mulberry I have found myself time and again returning to this source of inspiration. The campaign collection I created for Mulberry Home was inspired by the long-drawn-out military campaigns of the 19th century, when the British army took their families, and their collapsible furniture, with them.

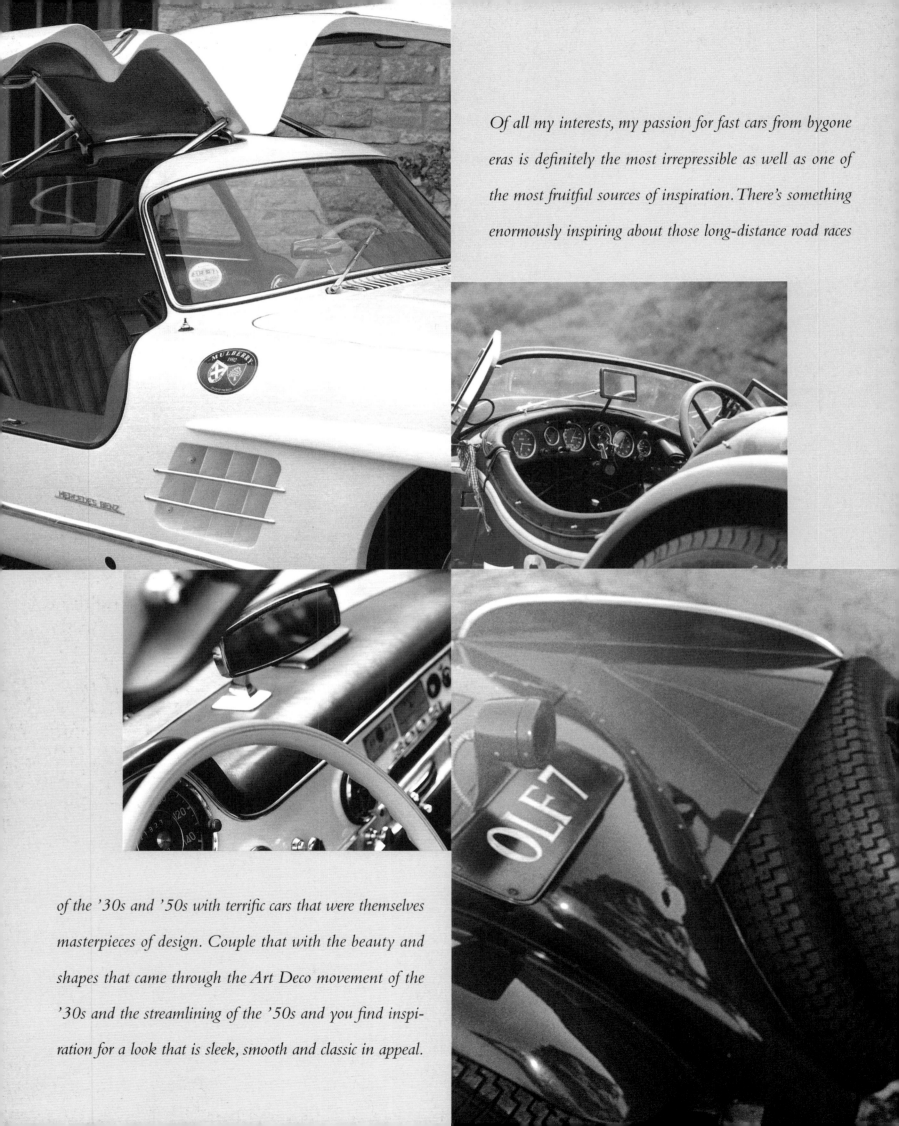

Of all my interests, my passion for fast cars from bygone eras is definitely the most irrepressible as well as one of the most fruitful sources of inspiration. There's something enormously inspiring about those long-distance road races of the '30s and '50s with terrific cars that were themselves masterpieces of design. Couple that with the beauty and shapes that came through the Art Deco movement of the '30s and the streamlining of the '50s and you find inspiration for a look that is sleek, smooth and classic in appeal.

It is not just the sport of sailing that I find exciting, it's all that goes with it. The particular quality of light found on or near water, the bleached colours, the specially made clothing, and above all the beauty, grandeur and timeless appeal of the sea itself. Nautical influences are never far away for our spring/summer collections, whether it's the use of canvas and eyelets, nautical maps, brass instruments or just amazingly shaped wooden flotsam. One of the best experiences I've had was helping great friends of ours decorate the interior of their yacht, which turned out to be a valuable discipline. Creating an interior within very tight confines, and yet conscious of the need also to be luxurious, trains you to concentrate on the truly important.

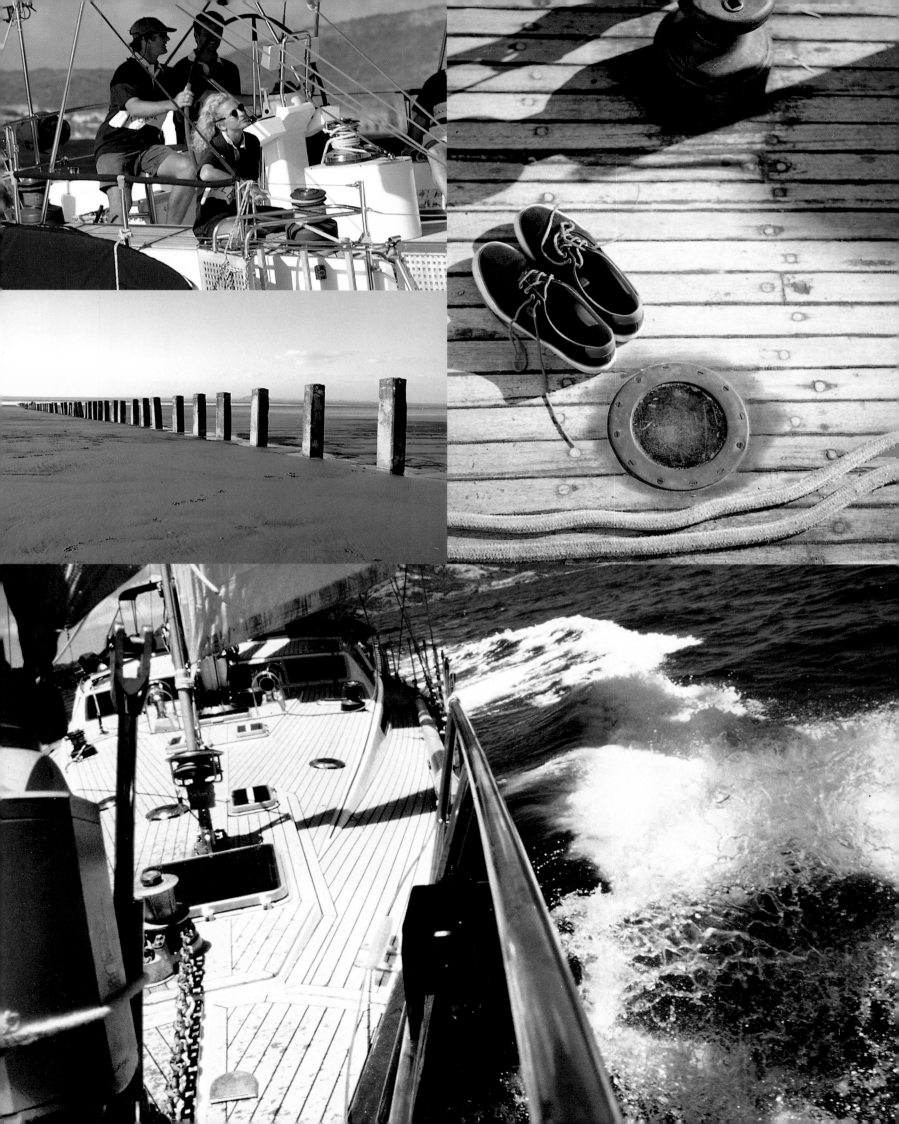

A love of gardens may seem to sit oddly with a passion for yachts and motor racing, but gardening holds every bit as much fascination for me and probably is one of my greatest influences. Among my earliest memories are those of my grandmother leading me around her wonderful gardens pointing out plants with exotic Latin names. My desire to return to the herbaceous borders of my youth remained dormant until I possessed a garden of my own. As a design challenge, planning a garden is unequalled – you have colour, texture, shape and season to wrestle with simultaneously. Just like building a collection, you have to wait six months to a year to bring your ideas to fruition, often only to find that the elements have ideas of their own!

INSPIRATIONS

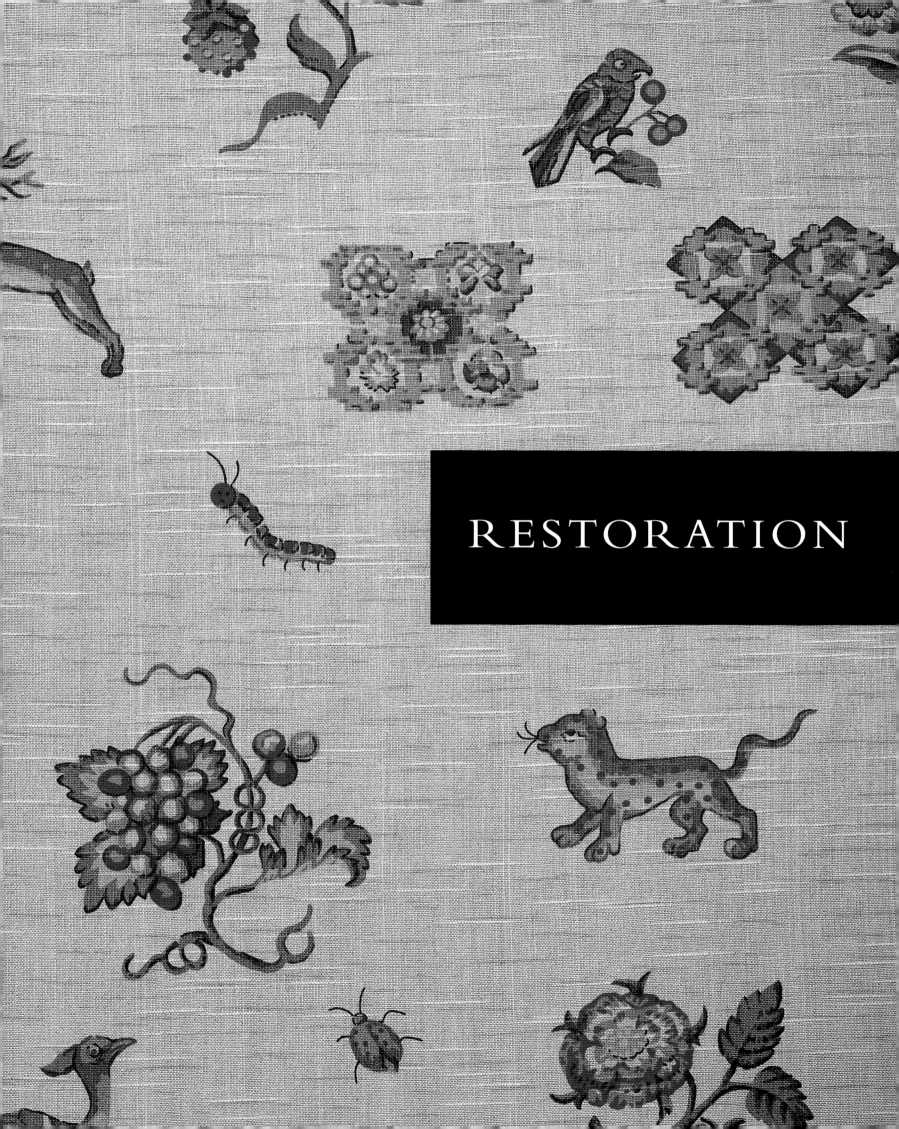

RESTORATION

This is the look with which we launched Mulberry Home, and it has remained popular ever since. The secret of its success, in my opinion, is the way in which the colours and fabrics blend seamlessly with collected antiques and objets trouvés. The rich but subtle colour palette of soft reds, golds, blues, green and naturals, combines with a strong emphasis on quality and craftsmanship. The fabrics themselves — warm chenilles, slubby linens and silks — are soft and very luxurious. People just love to touch them.

My inspirations for this look were both direct and indirect — direct as a result of discovering a fragment of fabric unearthed from a hidden fireplace, which inspired the Tudor Animals design (see preceding page); indirect in my love of ruined abbeys,

illuminated manuscripts, and the rich colours of Tudor costumes and paintings. My own house, a 14th-century English manor, was originally decorated in this style and it became the setting for much of our early publicity. I was astonished by the emotional response it evoked, seeming to offer a feeling of security

and tradition. In fact, this was the beginning of Mulberry Home. From the response to the decoration of our shops, which was very much modelled on our home, I realized that people wanted exactly the same interiors themselves — relaxed, friendly, good-looking but not demanding.

Our Restoration collection works particularly well in a country setting, where anything too brilliant or brash would jar when seen against the

quieter colours of nature, but can also work splendidly in the city. It looks particularly good with natural wood, especially the slightly golden tones of oak that has been oiled or waxed to produce a subtle sheen. Warm and inviting, it is also dog- and child-friendly – another reason for its popularity!

IRISH SUMMER

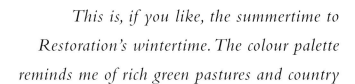

This is, if you like, the summertime to Restoration's wintertime. The colour palette reminds me of rich green pastures and country produce. To capture its flavour, think of the almost edible dairy colours of cream and buttermilk, the ancient walled gardens of great houses, overgrown and neglected, and the quiet unobtrusive charm of the Irish countryside.

We built this collection around soft, almost faded floral linens, unions and cottons, together with Donegal tweeds, and mixed them eclectically with design ideas from more exotic locations, such as a cream Melchior chenille and our Trevelyan silk panels, which look as though they have been in a fine Irish country house for generations. This quality of faded elegance and quite unobtrusive charm is quintessentially Irish.

This collection is ideally suited to large, light rooms – the kind of décor that Nancy Lancaster favoured – and makes smaller rooms instantly feel much more spacious. It has a 'Who's for tennis?' feel to it with its pale colours and summery charm. Light waxed pine floorboards, half-panelled walls, muslin voiles at the windows, deckchairs in soft stripes, self-patterns in smooth fabrics and simple campaign chairs all form part of this elegant but easy-going look. Although primarily inspired by the countryside, this relaxed yet simple look translates well into modern town houses, for example, where there is a growing trend to create unsophisticated, easy-to-live-with interiors that are minimalist without appearing either clinical or cold.

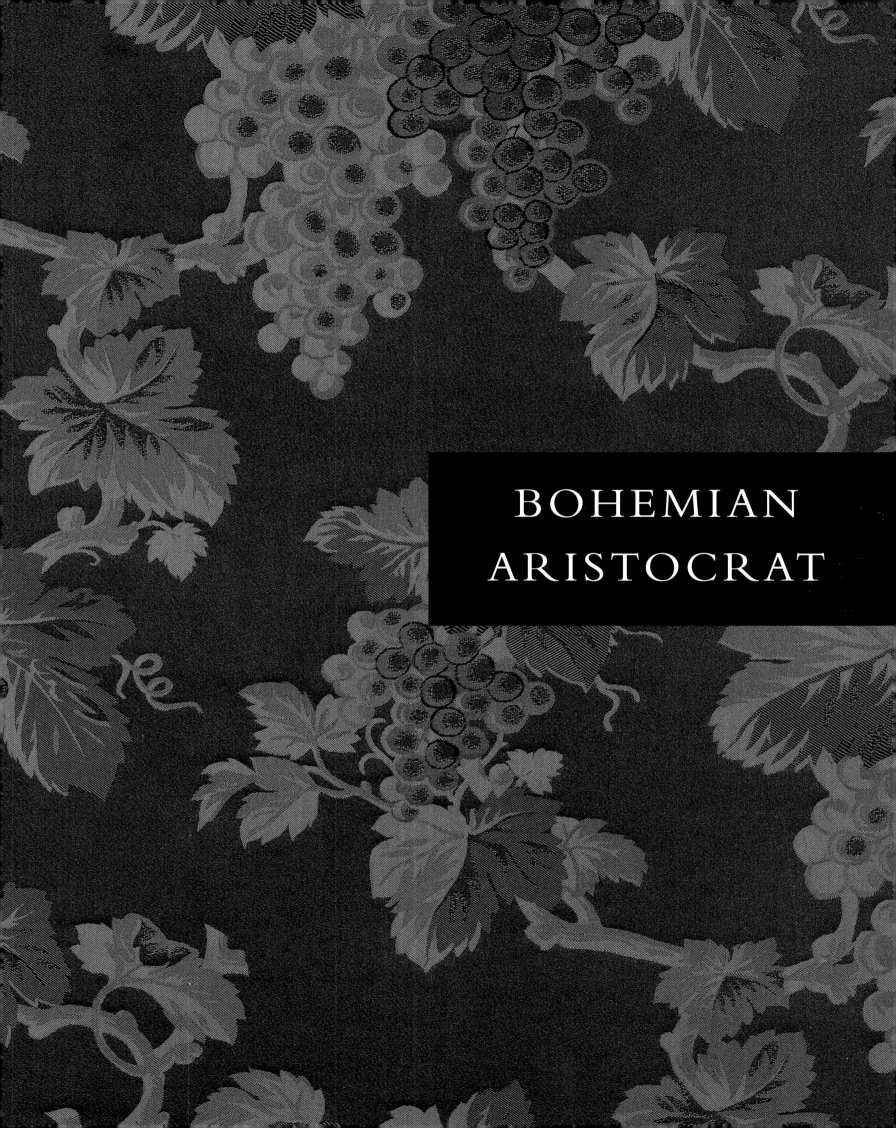

BOHEMIAN ARISTOCRAT

This is the raffish cousin of the Restoration look – altogether a bit more glamorous, exotic and daring, but definitely related! It is really my favourite. Our inspiration began with the Arab Hall in Lord Leighton's house in Kensington – built around the turn of the century when so many artists became enraptured with the

East and all things exotic. The deep, rich colour palette so beloved by pre-Raphaelite painters – with its rich colours of grape, ruby, gold and pewter – also fascinated us. Our fabric designs in this look – Mihrab, Paisley and Persian Tile – come straight from Moroccan or Middle Eastern interiors. The fabrics are exciting – deep-piled velvets, soft chenilles, luxurious silks, all with

embellishing touches of gold and silver tassels, fringes and braids. What brought it all to life, however, was our research into Diaghilev's designs for the Ballet Russe of St. Petersburg, for its European tour. The ever more sensuous and risqué productions were inspired by costumes from India and Persia. At much

the same time that we were getting the ideas for this collection together, I was in a 'colourist' period in my garden – learning to use tonal harmonies rather than contrasts to design the borders. Deep blues merging with violets through to Bordeaux reds, highlighted with touches of silver… the Bohemian Aristocrat colour palette in microcosm! This look is ideal for any young-at-heart country house or to give a town apartment the appeal of a Parisian artist's studio.

ROOM
AT THE TOP

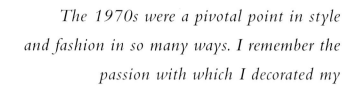

The 1970s were a pivotal point in style and fashion in so many ways. I remember the passion with which I decorated my own 'minimalist' Ladbroke Gardens apartment: white walls, Frank Martin prints, Bang and Olufsen TV and stereo, smoked glass and chrome coffee table, cream herringbone

linen sofa and leather beanbag, given an extra flourish with an 18th-century oak gateleg table and Chippendale country chairs.

What goes around comes around, and this particular collection echoes this theme, with its mix of design features from different eras – the '30s and '50s, as well as the '70s. By chance our administrative headquarters at Kilver Court in Somerset has some amazing rooms on the top

floor that are pure '50's minimalism, and they became part of the inspiration for this collection.

In this revamped look, we have used earth tones — off-white, coffee, mocha and ebony — and naturally smooth-textured materials, such as leather, iron, aluminium, wood and linen. Clean, spare lines are essential to this look, and the steel and leather rocking chairs, the leather beanbag and the wood-block table give it its essential flavour.

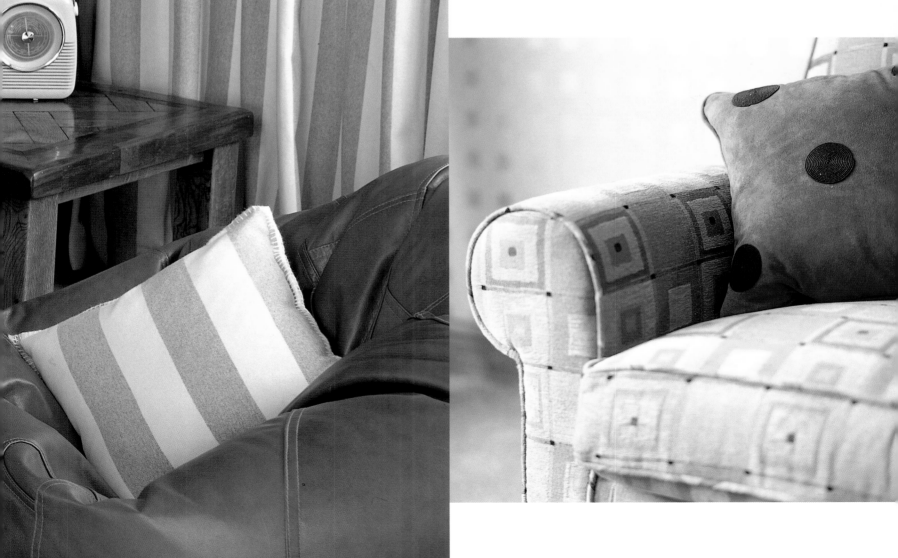

POOL PARTY

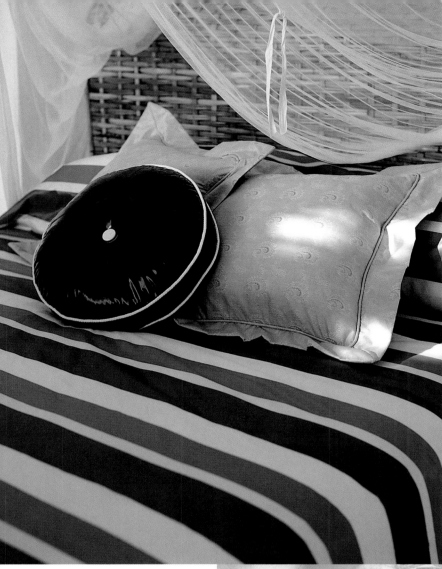

I have always loved the glamour of the film 'High Society', in which all the action takes place around the pool, and it is the atmosphere conjured up by these words which prompted this look. Its key notes are relaxed sophistication, and fun. Colours and fabrics are cool and fresh, with influences from the '50s. The colour palette is principally a clear, strong blue and white. Bold floral prints, like Rhode Island Roses, mix with strong contemporary spots and wide deckchair stripes. Fabrics include simple thick sailcloths and cotton piqué combined with others with a much more sheeny finish, such as glazed cotton chintzes and even PVC. Furniture and fittings have similar contrasts — rough wicker sits next to polished chrome, concrete and glass.

COUNTRY

English Manor House

THE 14TH-CENTURY stone manor house in which my wife, Monty, and I have lived with our children for the last 19 years is more than a home: it is a major source of inspiration for me; my first collections for Mulberry were very much inspired by its traditions, architecture and history.

If you are lucky enough, as we have been, to own a house with such a strong personality of its own, you will find that this governs the choices you make for the colour

ABOVE *The kitchen is a family room – and the heart of the house. Anyone working at the sink gets the benefit of marvellous views across the countryside.*

RIGHT *Equally important in a family house is a place where everyone can relax in real comfort. Capacious sofas are covered in a bold mix of patterns.*

ABOVE *In the entrance hall, we have exploited the walls for a collection of our favourite prints, while an equally loved collection of hats hangs on the antlers of a stag.*

LEFT *This is the dining hall – the grandest room in the house – where the harpsichord I gave Monty for her birthday has pride of place by the window. The painted detail inside the harpsichord's lid inspired our Pheasants and Urns fabric.*

RIGHT *One of the great advantages of subtle patterns like Pheasants and Urns is that they combine so easily with others in the same tonal range.*

palette, the style of furniture and the entire atmosphere of the interior.

The key elements are harmony and integrity. We have tried to use a toning colour palette where the fabrics and colours look, if not faded, at least as if they have lived with the house. The furniture has strong lines in solid timber whilst the upholstery is generously stuffed – nothing looks worse than mean or skimped padding.

'The look is noticeably dog-eared and even more noticeably dog-friendly', wrote Christopher Petkanas

ABOVE *An antique wing chair, covered in Paisley Stripe, in front of the library window at which our Golden Lily bedspread has been hung as a curtain. These soft and rich patterns used together create a 'lived in' look.*

RIGHT *The windows in the music room have been dressed with old rose Baccarat silk (the reverse side of the fabric used for the borders) while the library chair is resplendent in Aubusson chenille in soft creams, pinks and greens, and the high-back occasional chair is covered in Proud Lions.*

FAR RIGHT *It is vitally important that this type of house looks lived in and as though it has been there for ever. One of the challenges in an old house is to ensure that any new introductions do not jar by looking too modern. The bookshelves in the library are a recent addition but, by choosing wood from a reclamation yard, we have managed to create the impression that they are a long-standing fixture. One of my favourite ways to soften the look in a room is to use throws and panels on chairs and sofas, as here. You can 'lift' a colour scheme or make a room appear more lived-in, using beautiful pieces of fabric for this purpose.*

TOP LEFT *Thanks to the vagaries of the weather, a garden room is bound to be a much-used place for sitting and relaxing. Ours is no exception!*

RIGHT *This little terrace is the ideal sheltered spot for a drink after a swim.*

FAR RIGHT *Teenagers need their own space. Old motor rally posters decorate this teenager's den, giving it a 'Boys Own' flavour.*

LEFT *The dining hall, seen from the minstrel's gallery, is the ultimate party room, and has seen a lot of service. On the great refectory table in the centre, Balcony brocade makes an attractive table runner. Appropriately, Medieval panels hang at the windows and – a touch of the court jester – Pierrot spot chenille covers the dining chairs.*

in a review of the house for *Architectural Digest*. 'Deeply buttoned Chesterfield sofas are draped with chenille throws. Colonial chairs in weathered willow cradle bullion-embroidered cushions'. Since that review we have gone on to embrace a number of different collections, but my favourite remains Bohemian Aristocrat with its combinations of deep rich colours.

LEFT *The Tudor Animals fabric on the headboard of the bed in our guestroom was inspired by a fragment of cloth found behind panelling when we were restoring the house, while one of our Intaglia panels doubles up as a bedspread.*

BELOW *I am very fond of our campaign-style chairs – this one doubles up as a bedroom chair.*

Elements of Design

Paying attention to small touches, to exquisite craftsmanship and beautiful finishing detail, is what gives an interior character and charm. I love the small drawers of a bureau, the sensuous feel of cushions, the generous curves of a Victorian roll top bath, heavy silverware and good quality crystal, traditional English bone china, the artistry of well-designed shelving and storage, neatly hidden from sight in a walk in cupboard, and last but not least, the texture of walnuts against the smooth silvery sheen of a pewter plate. Together, these sum up the mood and atmosphere of traditional England.

Dutch Farmhouse

THE MOMENT YOU step over the threshold of this Dutch farmhouse, you immediately feel at home. Welcoming and relaxing, no element of its design or furnishing jars or feels out of place. Wonderful antiques, large comfortable sofas, generous hangings and soft candlelight combine to give the house a feeling of long-standing tradition, very much in keeping with its strong country roots and sturdy functional past. The architecture, with its square rooms downstairs and its sloping barn-style

ABOVE *The drawing room has a soft, gentle charm and elegant simplicity in shades of cream and rose. Wide waxed floorboards provide a country-style floor, with a kelim in rose and gold providing the only splash of colour. The hangings at the windows provide a touch of luxury.*

RIGHT *A magnificent carved 18th-century oak table, set on a Chinese rug, makes a feature in this hallway with its handsome stone-paved floor.*

LEFT *The master bedroom cleverly uses contrasting textures with a variety of Mulberry fabrics in toning shades. The boarded, plain-painted ceiling is offset by the delicate lace hangings of the four poster and richly patterned window panels.*

TOP *An antique free-standing bath and washstand lend character to the small bathroom under the eaves, while the tartan rug adds a welcome splash of colour.*

ABOVE *The dressing room uses subtle colour harmonies of golds, creams and rose. The chair is upholstered in Persian Tiles whilst the curtains are Paisley.*

bedrooms upstairs, adds character and variety, while the simple wooden, stone or tiled floors and plain painted pale walls provide a more modern touch.

The Hartmann family, who own the farmhouse, manage the Mulberry shops in Amsterdam. They value their country's heritage of richly carved antiques and fine architecture but they also enjoy the simplicity of up-to-date

LEFT This corner of the kitchen has a medieval feel, with its simple flagged floors, pale walls and antique furniture. The antique distressed cupboard and provides a great deal of useful storage (above). The dining chair is a typical country design found in Holland.

RIGHT The working area of the kitchen, with its hand-made fitted cupboards, painted in soft cream, is light and spacious while retaining its farmhouse appeal, thanks to the traditional range and table.

styling: for the Hartmann family, Mulberry furnishings provide just the bridge required between old and new. The family's ability to use the best of the old and bring it up to date is what makes this house so special – providing stability and security but managing to remain fresh and unstuffy at the same time.

Pale paint on the walls in off-white, beige and cream makes the house appear light and spacious, and provides a foil for the pieces of dark wood furniture. For the soft furnishings, Vera and John have opted for subtle shifts of colour which blend seamlessly with each other and are enhanced by the way in which patterns have been varied.

LEFT *A circular marble-topped dining table under the glowing light of an antique crystal chandelier makes an attractive eating area. It is at once both formal, with its luxurious use of marble and crystal, and informal, with the addition of director's chairs rather than conventional dining chairs.*

ABOVE *When open, the generously sized double doors to the dining room enable this area to form part of the living space when required.*

RIGHT *As an alternative to the traditional range, the farmhouse kitchen also houses a modern gas cooker. The polished stainless steel cooker hood and centrally positioned island work station similarly lend a distinctly contemporary touch.*

ABOVE *The master bedroom demonstrates Vera's taste for mixing old and new. Sharply tailored fine calico Roman blinds create a light filtering screen for the large windows, while the bed sports an eclectic mixture of Mulberry throws and tartan rugs, as well as traditional style tapestry cushions, in softly toning shades.*

Elements of Design

The mixing of soft warm fabrics with stylish architectural detail is one of the distinguishing features of this easy-to-live-with look. Cool floor tiles and neatly tailored upholstery complement the hand-crafted pottery and Renaissance-style fabrics, used in small touches, for throws, footstools and cushions. Gold-braiding and thick fringing embellish

the heavy fabrics, which are luxurious and soft to the touch, to provide a decorative accent. Combining a variety of patterns is another strong element in this look: tartans of many different plaids and colours sit in happy juxtaposition with other bold geometrical prints to create a swathe of blazing colour. These brightly coloured woollen fabrics make a cosy corner, which is living proof of its dog-friendly appeal.

Country House Hotel

DECORATED IN COUNTRY house style, Charlton House Hotel evokes the effortless atmosphere of a weekend house party from a bygone area. What is not so obvious is that this homely weekend retreat has to accommodate the wear and tear of around ten thousand people a year passing though its doors. Creating the appropriate decor to meet such demands was a major challenge but I bought Charlton House Hotel not just to restore it to its former glory, but to make it even more special.

From the guests' point of view, however, the hotel must be a place of sanctuary and a home from home. Our Restoration and Bohemian Aristocrat looks are ideal for this purpose. Old dark wood, rich, soft fabrics in subtly varied patterns, well-upholstered furniture, glowing Persian carpets and Turkish kelims all form part of its appeal.

ABOVE *The grounds around the hotel features some magnificent old trees, like this ancient beech – the shade is ideal for tea on the lawns.*

TOP RIGHT *The generous curves of the staircase give the hotel a splendid Edwardian elegance. Dark painted walls are ideal for displaying a print collection.*

RIGHT AND FAR RIGHT *Looking through into the hotel's drawing room (right), the lacrosse sticks and fishing rods create a family feel to the entrance hall (far right).*

TOP LEFT *A pitched roof adds character to one of the bedrooms, furnished in simple country style. Windows look out onto the beautiful grounds.*

BOTTOM LEFT *Crisp white bedlinen and jugs of fresh flowers make any bedroom more inviting. The bedhead here is covered in one of our all-time favourite fabrics, Ancient Mulberry Tartan.*

LEFT *Each room at Charlton House Hotel is individual. In this, one of the more sumptuous bedrooms, a magnificent carved four poster bed creates a stunning central feature. Dark walls, luxurious soft fabrics on the chairs and our Mulberry panels doubling as bedspreads give the room a truly royal atmosphere.*

Elements of Design

Inherent in this rich and sumptuous look are a whole host of decorative elements, from furniture to fabrics, glassware and china, and passementerie. The choice of a deep-bordered gold braid on a velvet cushion, a lacquered gold band on a Venetian style claret glass, a golden silk tassel for a curtain tie-back or a thick gold fringe for a cushion, add up to an overall feeling of sumptuous splendour.

The fabric patterns softly harmonize, with a mixture of traditional damask patterns, checks and 'teardrop' Paisleys in soft reds, greens, blues and golds. The traditional Paisley pattern – one of Mulberry's best loved fabrics – originally emanated from India, and this particular look has overtones of the last days of the Raj with its combination of ruby reds and burnished golds.

Dutch Manor House

STYLISH YET SIMPLE, this elegant 18th-century Dutch manor house provides the backdrop for its owner's indefatigable enthusiasm for interior design. No sooner has Suzanne Loggere, the distributor of Mulberry in Holland, decorated a room than she starts to think of new ways of arranging it! It is just this element of novelty and surprise that gives the house its particular charm; its owner is particularly gifted at finding unusual ways to display *objets d'art* and of mixing modern design ideas with traditional Dutch decoration. Luxurious yet simple, homely without being plain, it combines several of Mulberry's looks with effortless ease.

ABOVE *The secluded 18th-century manor house with its hipped, tiled roof, is typical of the period.*

LEFT *A deep-blue decorative motif adorns the simple lime-washed table and benches in the basement, whilst the embroidered cushions introduce a nautical element.*

FAR LEFT *With its jaunty nautical air, the blue and white living room is smart yet simple. The panelled white-painted walls contrast the deep blue frieze which encircles the room at ceiling height, and is reminiscent of a ship's pennant. Very much part of this theme, Mulberry's own nautical flag fabric is used for the upholstered stool cum coffee table, and for cushions on the deep blue sofas.*

TOP LEFT *Cosy, warm and inviting, the colour scheme of the sitting room focuses on soft golds, pinks and rusts. Honey-coloured waxed floorboards give the room a natural, simple country feel, while rich-coloured Mulberry fabrics are used for the upholstered stool, folding chair and cushions.*

BELOW LEFT *The comfortable two-seater Chesterfield upholstered in a traditional Floral Rococo print and the folding card table set for tea create a similarly intimate, cosy feel to this interior, with its wonderful fireplace and typically Dutch stove.*

LEFT *This corner demonstrates the restrained elegance of Suzanne's decorative ideas, with its generously draped tall windows.*

Elements of Design

Cool, soft colours and modern styling combined with heirloom pieces epitomise this look. It is feminine, gentle and singularly easy to live with, and works as well in town as in country settings. An eye for good form, interesting textures and toning colours is the key. Here the handsome lines of an old wing chair are accentuated by an off-white slubbed fabric; matching distressed white clay pots are ideal plant holders; silverware and china are traditional; elegant wicker plant holders embellish a mantelpiece; silky cushions dress up a plain sofa and yet more plants adorn a simple wooden kitchen table.

SEABOARD

Florida Beach House

WASHED BY THE Gulf of Mexico, and built on sand, this spectacular house in Florida belongs to close friends of mine. It is an unusual architectural combination: the rear part, facing the sea, is ultra-modern while the front porch is unashamedly colonial in style.

Inside the house is wonderfully light and airy. The open-plan design, with its cathedral ceilings and cool floors, makes maximum use of any refreshing sea breezes – a must in this part of the world where the summers are unbelievably hot and humid.

Light and space are the hallmarks of this house; one of its major features is a breezeway overlooking the pool while another is the terraces which open out from almost every room. We visit often as a family, and luxuriate in the light and space; watching the sunset over the Gulf, banana daiquiri in hand, is a special delight.

Cool fabrics like cotton and linen are a must in a climate as hot and sticky as this is, while smooth surfaces are not only cool but in keeping with the free-flowing architectural style. Although it is possible

RIGHT *The loose-covered dining chairs, moved out onto the balcony for an al fresco meal, are covered in a mixture of Mulberry fabrics including Rhode Island Roses, the bold diagonals of Tipsy Stripe and Soda Spot in navy. The blue and white theme is very much in keeping with the beach-house setting.*

to use pattern, too much of it would detract from the clean, simple lines of the house: small touches of bright pattern work best.

The house has a refreshing mixture of old and new; pride of place goes to a Wurlitzer jukebox while a pair of antique Indian doors form part of a specially constructed cupboard. These interesting pieces of furniture have the same impact in this ultra-modern white space as a painting or piece of sculpture.

ABOVE *A single wicker chair, with Charleston check seat pad, marks the corner between the living space and the breezeway overlooking the pool.*

RIGHT *A giant sofa, also in Charleston check, looks out towards the sea. The concrete floor beneath is actually made from ground-up seashells.*

THIS PAGE *The PVC navy/white and white/navy cushions look absolutely right with the clean lines of the Philippe Starck-style table and chairs on the terrace overlooking the ocean.*

FAR LEFT *Behind the sofa, with its full complement of cushions in Mulberry fabrics, is the cupboard I gave Detlef for his birthday. I bought the doors in India, and Detlef then had the cupboard made up around them. Antiques like this, carefully positioned, make an excellent counterpoint to the uncompromising modern style of the house.*

LEFT *The simple cream sofa sits at one end of the master bedroom, with clean modern lines and Solitaire cushions.*

BELOW *The bathroom adjoining the master bedroom is cleverly hidden behind a semi-partition wall. Simple, cool and functional, it is exactly what is required for the hot and sultry climate.*

Elements of Design

Clean lines within a simple white and blue colour scheme is the key to this sunny, light, beachside look, which could be translated into any house with good natural light and fair-sized rooms. Simple stripes and checks form the basic patterns on towels, tablecloths and cushions, such as Tipsy Stripe for the table-cloth and Tattersall Check for the towels.

Pure polished pale wood, simple rounded chairs in natural beechwood or maple, or slightly rougher wicker, blend with it, giving a slightly '50s retro feel. Occasional touches of more sumptuous pattern, as in the Rhode Island Roses florals, help to soften the stark white lines of the house. Contrasts of form — the rounded shapes of armchairs and basins — create a much needed contrast with the tough lines of the architecture.

Istanbul Apartment

INFLUENCED BY THE architecture of local mosques and palaces with their domes and minarets, Asli Gunisray has created a magnificent blend of east and west in an apartment with uncompromisingly modern architecture. Crammed with a wonderful collection of artefacts from Turkey's imperial past, this apartment is also home to a great many disparate pieces from France, England, China and Russia.

A true cosmopolitan, Asli is particularly clever in the way she mixes and matches periods and cultures with her collection of Mulberry pieces into this eclectic background. Asli mixes Mulberry fabrics with aplomb, combining rich red and golden chenilles and silks with red Chinese lacquer and black Mandarin hat boxes, while very English Longton Hall china sits with dignity on an old Turkish leather trunk doubling up as a coffee table. The jostling lively combination of pieces is a faithful reflection of life in this great capital city, one of the fastest growing in the world.

LEFT *Asli's living room, with its truly magnificent views, gives pride of place to Turkish artefacts, including a splendid antique carved coffer and a handsome Turkish rug.*

RIGHT *Seen here from across the Golden Horn, the Galata Tower stands proud against the Istanbul skyline, and is part of the stunning seaview enjoyed from Asli's apartment.*

LEFT *A particularly fine inlaid Turkish coffer provides the piece de resistance in the principal living room. Its handsome polished lid provides a useful showcase for Asli's collection of personal mementos.*

Elements of Design

To create the soukh-like atmosphere of this apartment, deep rich colours have been used both for the walls and for the furnishings. The exotic eastern feel is enhanced with touches of glamour from exquisite Turkish antiques, including heavily carved wooden furniture and doors and beautifully wrought copper coffee pots and lanterns.

CITY

Apartment Block

FROM OUR FIRST meeting, when he bought one of our Donegal suits, Sir Bob Geldof has become one of the most unlikely yet most photographed ambassadors Mulberry has ever had. He actually has an extremely well-developed sense of style in both dress and interior design. One of the first to embrace our Bohemian Aristocrat look, he has now opted for

ABOVE *The '30s style Eltham sofa covered in Pierrot spot chenille makes a simple statement against one wall in the living room, whilst a pleated lampshade creates an elegant contrast.*

LEFT *Coffee and taupe create a simple colour palette. The sweeping curve of the sofa with its natural linen cover makes a textural contrast with the sumptuous silky folds of the Magic Circles curtains.*

RIGHT *The polished wood '70s sideboard, the soft leather folds of the Mulberry beanbag and the glossy leather of the buttoned '50s chair are a subtle mixture of contrasting forms and harmonizing surfaces, set off by the polished wooden sculptures on the sideboard.*

the cool urban chic of our Room at the Top range for his London apartment. The colour scheme he has chosen – creamy white with rich earth and wood tones – ensures that the apartment looks warm and inviting but superbly uncluttered. What pattern there is tends to be geometric and almost monochrome in colour, giving the rooms a '70s look with a '90s twist – Bob calls it his 'hip-jazz' look!

Modern furniture with clean lines is ideal for this look. Sir Bob has opted for comfortable sofas with neatly contoured shapes, simple chairs with clearly defined wooden legs and for one of our most successful recent additions – the leather beanbag.

RIGHT *The bathroom adjoining the master bedroom demonstrates brilliantly the subtle mixture of dark surfaces with a simple white background, where purity of form can be seen at its best.*

Elements of Design

*Texture is the key to this look in every form –
polished wood, rough sisal carpet, silk fabrics,
suede and leather in rich tones of cream, tan,
coffee, mocha, black and white. Pattern is graphic,
generous and equally simple with a limited colour
palette, whilst self-texturing plays a major part, as
in the Pierrot spot chenille in a soft mushroom on
the Eltham sofa and the suede Spiral cushions.*

Mews House

WITH ITS GOTHIC-INSPIRED decor, the coach house belonging to John Leslie proves that you can divide large rooms into intimate living spaces using strong colours and bold combinations. John, together with our interior designer Jackie Jones, used a mixture of rich, deep and exotic colours to create an embracing, comfortable feel to the interior.

ABOVE *Comfortable sofas provide the seating, with a footstool upholstered in Daisy Daisy chenille serving as an occasional table. Pillars with Mulberry panels divide the room from a television area below.*

LEFT *Here a large Knole sofa, enlivened with Jester silk and woven Pointer cushions, and an Indian coffee table with a Muscat Grapes runner create a comfortable corner.*

RIGHT *The dining room, which doubles as the conservatory, has a rich Renaissance feel to it, thanks to the elegance of the gilt-rimmed ornate Imperial glassware and richly patterned Longton Hall china.*

Elements of Design

Exotic pattern, luxurious texture and deep colours are the key elements in creating this look. In a small space, you can afford to go to town on luxury fabrics, and they have been used here for sofas, wall panels, runners, cushions and bedspreads in a mixture of velvets and wool weaves – soft fabrics with a wonderfully tactile quality. Elegant china and glassware complete the look.

A carved oak Mulberry bed covered in a luxurious crushed velvet bedspread and an array of scatter cushions makes an enticing retreat. Panels with Jacobean-style prints of fleur-de-lys, crowns and pineapples are used to divide up the space – a flower arrangement picks up the colours. Gilt-edged crystal and heavily embossed silver cutlery add to the air of opulence.

Warehouse Loft

Hᴵɢʜ ᴀʙᴏᴠᴇ ᴛʜᴇ busy streets of central London, the sixth-floor apartment belonging to photographer David Bailey and his wife Catherine demonstrates how the traditional and modern can combine with wit and style. As part of a residential development created from a former factory, the uncompromising architecture of the apartment reveals its industrial roots. Plain brick and bare plaster walls, together with huge

Aʙᴏᴠᴇ *A handsome antique roll top bath sits next to a comfortable, well-upholstered armchair – bathrooms don't have to be clinical.*

Rɪɢʜᴛ *The brick walls provide a textural contrast to the sensuous forms of the Buddhist figures and silky fabrics of the curtains and footstool.*

THIS PAGE *The master bedroom with its Golden Paisley headboard and a Kailiff woven panel on the bed. The bedside lamp, with its turned wood base, has a shade in Muscat Grapes fabric.*

glazed areas, provide the basic framework while the furniture is an eclectic mixture of period pieces from the Bailey's former home in Primrose Hill, sculpture from foreign travels and several Mulberry pieces from different collections.

The main living area is predominantly brick and tan in colour, echoing the mellow tones of the highly polished wooden boards of the floor.

In the bedrooms, rich colours predominate with soft and luxurious velvets and chenilles in burgundy and gold. Geometric patterns in stripes, checks and spots in harmonizing tones add lustre and texture. The statuary, carved Indian furniture and relics blend into this ultra-modern setting, thanks to the link provided by these exotic fabrics and furniture.

LEFT *A Knole sofa in Ribbon Stripe alongside Mulberry's leather and steel rocking chair – one of the key pieces from the Room at the Top collection.*

Elements of Design

This apartment is as much about texture as it is about pattern, and the most adaptable fabric is leather, which can look soft and relaxed or lean and tailored depending on the form that it takes. Here, in the sensuously moulded beanbag and in the well-stuffed frame of the two-seater sofa, it links the simplicity of the basic brick wall and polished wooden floorboards to the more sumptuous fabrics and furnishings of the rest of the apartment.

Victorian Town House

CLASSICAL WITH A modern twist, there is a lightness and elegant beauty about this London town house that is very feminine. It comes as no surprise to find that it belongs to Darcey Bussell, one of England's favourite prima ballerinas, whom I met when she was performing in La Bayadayère at Covent Garden.

Her house has some splendid architectural features, including a handsome marble fireplace, elaborately carved cornices, large windows and original old pine floorboards, which needed a simple but elegant scheme in softly toning neutral colours to set them off to advantage.

A slightly baroque touch can be found in the choice of fabrics – the soft creams and yellows often decorated with a touch of gold lend an air of luxury. The result is an interior with a sunny, relaxed atmosphere with a hint of theatricality. Generous curves of sofas and armchairs echo the curling and scrolling architectural detail, while the huge elaborately carved gilded mirror above the fireplace in the living room forms a bridge between the architecture and the interior scheme.

ABOVE *Moss stitch circle and velvet cushions dress up the sofa.*

LEFT *The pale tones of this interior coupled with the traditional forms of the furniture create a look that is antique yet modern, classical but young at heart. Flowing creams, golds and beiges add warmth to the colour scheme, while rich wood tones punctuate the otherwise neutral setting. Elegant fabrics abound: the sofa is upholstered in Chenille Squares, whilst the large stool is in Magic Circles.*

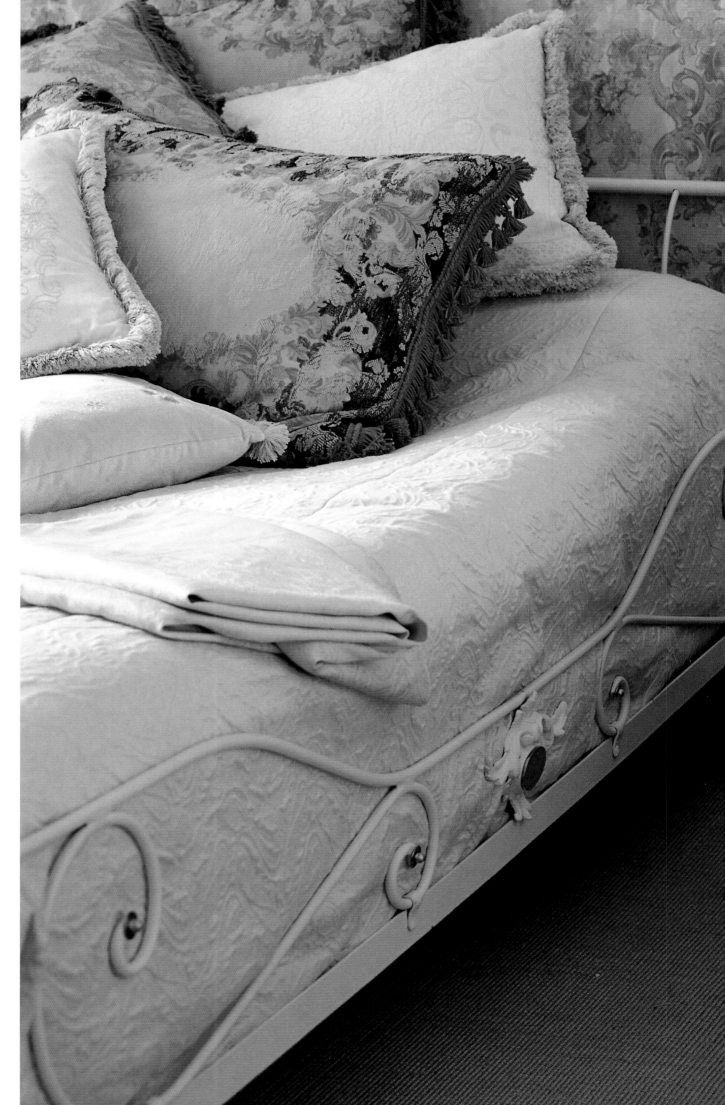

RIGHT *The Sleigh bed has a Matelasse bedspread in Paisley pattern, while the Lansdown chair is covered in Bayadayère. A Trevelyan panel hangs behind the bed.*

Elements of Design

Softly traditional and sumptuously elegant, this look is the perfect complement for turn of the century architecture, be it a Paris apartment or a London townhouse, without the heaviness normally associated with it. Pale colours, such as gold, beige, ecru and cream, and sleek fabrics, such as silks, brocades and damasks, are concentrated with sensuously curved forms, be it the ornately carved arms of a chair or the ends of a bed or in the lines of a traditional English bone-china teapot. Candlelight, with its soft golden intimate glow, brings out its depth and sets this look off to perfection. Small, exquisite finishing touches complete the look and give it its special appeal.

Georgian Town House

I T TAKES VISION and courage to turn a classic 19th-century interior into a showhouse of contemporary design, but this is exactly what Jane Artus, who designed the interior of this house for a client of Mulberry, has done. The secret of her success is the way in which she has allowed a generous feeling for space and architecture to dominate the design, which is eclectic but uncluttered. Bold use of strong colour is a feature of this house, and gives it a very modern twist.

ABOVE *The hallway is restrained, classical, cool and symmetrical. A great introduction to the architecture of the house.*

RIGHT *The drawing room houses an eclectic mix of antique and contemporary. Underneath the massive modern canvas, A Single Twin by Stephen Chambers, is one of Mulberry's traditional Knole sofas in shot velvet. Rich deep tones give this room warmth and intimacy.*

I particularly like the way Jane has used Mulberry classics in a fresh and unusual way; it has given me a new insight into how our fabrics and furnishings can be used. Deep coloured walls in strong royal blues, tobacco browns and clarets make a dramatic backdrop for the fabrics which contrast with each other – a Moroccan bed-drape in a deep shade of blue stands out against a burnt earth-coloured wall, giving it a North African feel.

ABOVE *In the family room, a modern version of Georgian stripes, our Ribbon Stripe fabric, covers the long sofa, while the chairs are in our popular tobacco coloured Tattersall Check.*

LEFT *More classical in tone, the elegant master bedroom has soft earth-coloured walls. Very architectural lamps from Jane's own company complement an equally elegant antique chaise longue upholstered in Muscat Grapes.*

LEFT *The true glamour of this house is seen in the magnificent dining room with its deep blue walls and massive Regency-style dining table and chairs. Shimmering silver and the handsome blue and white dinner service set off the table to perfection.*

OVERLEAF *A bath fit for a king! Set in front of this pair of Georgian windows, through which light is filtered by a delicate voile, this roll top bath has a sculptural beauty of its own, its glistening surface reflected in the cool limestone tiles.*

Bold positioning – the massive copper free-standing bath in front of a pair of beautiful Georgian windows or the siting of a large traditional sofa under an equally huge contemporary painting – are hall-marks of this house. Almost palatial in its conception, it is innovative yet deeply traditional. Great stuff!

ABOVE *The guest bedroom, with its kaftan-style bed, is covered with a Golden Paisley chenille throw and bullion cushions. The Moroccan-style hooded drapes (originally designed as a chair cover) gives the room a slightly eastern flavour, emphasized by the unusual colour scheme of ochre with midnight blue.*

Elements of Design

The elegant architectural detail is the principal feature in this Georgian town house, from the old skylight over the stairwell, through the sinuously curving staircase, down to the handsome proportions of the reception rooms. The clever use of space, coupled with fascinating contrasts – a large, colourful modern canvas juxtaposed by interesting twists and scrolls on lamp bases, fabric edgings and mirrors, for example –

give the design vibrancy and interest. Texture is a major element in this house, from the smooth limestone floors to rich chenille throws, from highly polished copper and steel to the rough twist of sisal carpeting. Coolly spacious but warmly inviting, classical yet modern, this highly individual look with its inherent contrasts is absolutely right for up-to-the-minute town house living.

Eltham Palace

A SUPREME EVOCATION of 1930's style and glamour, the Art Deco rooms at Eltham Palace have been lovingly restored to their original splendour by English Heritage, and were opened to the public in June 1999.

Having studied in detail the original materials used in Eltham Palace from existing records, the historians and researchers at English Heritage immediately approached Mulberry to supply the fabrics used in the restoration. Quite amazingly, our fabrics matched the originals almost exactly in design, colour and quality. Most importantly, however, English Heritage felt the Mulberry fabrics would help capture the exciting mood of the sophisticated lives of Stephen and Virigina Courtauld, the palace's original owners. With their numerous parties, weekend guests and exotic taste –

LEFT *The rotunda Entrance Hall makes a dramatic impact with its striking architecture. The form of the glazed dome is echoed by the distinctive circular rug beneath, and perfectly complements the walnut furniture reupholstered by Mulberry in cream Maze Matelasse.*

OVERLEAF *The sumptuous oval bedroom with its exquisitely veneered walls and decorative panelling is a masterpiece of '30s design.*

which included a pet lemur and Virginia's snake tattoo – life at Eltham was pleasureable in the extreme.

Stephen and Virginia Courtauld first discovered Eltham Palace when they were looking for a residence in London; as great patrons of the arts they wanted somewhere close to theatres, concert halls and film studios. They fell in love with the Great Hall at Eltham – the childhood home of Henry VIII – and took considerable pride in its restoration, whilst building the adjoining Art Deco rooms in the most avant garde style of the times. Their adventurous design included 'ocean liner' styling, contrasting marble, silver ceilings with concealed lighting, built-in sound systems and vacuum cleaners, blonde wood and leather panelling, black doors inlaid with silver animals (copied from drawings made at London Zoo) and a gold mosaic and onyx bathroom.

THIS PAGE *The Great Hall at Eltham Palace, the boyhood home of Henry VIII, has been restored to its former glory.*

Elements of Design

The quality of materials and workmanship, together with the exciting architecture, the symmetry of design and the generous proportions of each room, create a dramatic interior. The cool polished surfaces of marble and walnut veneer are contrasted with the warm textures of silks, velvets and matelasse. Colour schemes are mainly monochromatic – honey blonde and cream, or black, white and silver – with occasional touches of vibrant colour, such as the deep purples, reds and blues used in the drawing room. The simple repetition of design motifs, and the surprise of hidden or built-in features are further elements which make this Art Deco house very special. English Heritage have truly restored the palace to its former splendour.

MY LIST OF THANK YOUS could go on and on, so please forgive me if I've missed someone out, as really this is not so much just about the book – it's really the whole of Mulberry Home.

Jill Evans, without whom Mulberry Home would never have become the essence it is; *the worldwide Mulberry Home team* who's never ending enthusiasm has brought the collection to life; *Ian Jupp and the Charlton House team,* where we've learnt the reality of furnishing a beautiful but hard working hotel and restaurant; *David Bailey* for his inspirational foreword; all those who have allowed us to feature their wonderful homes within the book; the photographers who have become friends over the years; *Victoria Murray,* our tireless Mulbery Home PR who has literally "cemented" this book together for us; and so many more. But most of all *Monty,* my wife, who's retyped my jumbled mutterings on the computer until late at night and has been there for me so many times when the pressure was on.

Roger Saul

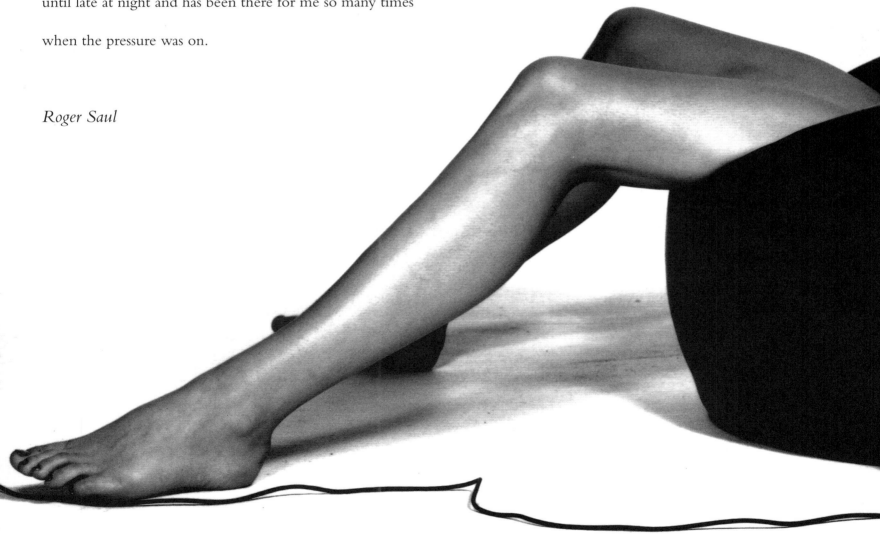

FABRICS AND FURNISHINGS *featured in this book are generally available from the Mulberry Home collection. Mulberry sells in over forty countries worldwide. For information on your nearest stockist please contact:*

Mulberry Home Customer Services
tel: + 44 (0)1761 234212
fax: + 44 (0)1761 233436
email: home@mulberry-england.co.uk

For trade enquiries please contact Mulberry Home Customer Services as listed above.

For fabric, wallpaper and trimmings in the USA distributed exclusively to the trade by:

Lee Jofa
Mulberry Home
tel: + 1 (516) 752 7600
fax: + 1 (516) 752 7623

For your nearest recommended interior designer or for the Mulberry Interior Design Service please contact Mulberry Home Customer Services as listed left.

Mulberry Headquarters
Kilver Court
Shepton Mallet
Somerset BA4 5NF
England
tel: + 44 (0)1749 340500
fax: + 44 (0)1749 345532
email: enquiries@mulberry-england.co.uk
http: www.mulberry-england.co.uk

Mulberry flagship store
41/42 New Bond Street
London W1
tel: + 44 (0)20 7491 3900

THE PUBLISHER THANKS the following photographers and organisations for their kind permission to reproduce the photographs in this book:

All photographs are by *Ebury Press/Bill Batten* unless otherwise stated:

7 *Simon Wilkinson*; 8 *Cheryl Koralick*; 9 *Peter Rosenbaum*; 10 *Ian Sumner*; 11 top left *Chris Dawn*; 11 bottom right *Ian Sumner*; 14 bottom *Rosemary Saul*; 16 top left *Ian Sumner*; 16 top right and bottom right *Cameron Saul*; 17 *Gerard D. Wagner*; 18 top left and top right *Peter Rosenbaum*; 18 bottom left *Stephen Colover*; 18 bottom right *Alexis Andrews*; 19 top left and bottom *Alexis Andrews*; 19 top right *Stephen Colover*; 20 top left *Nicola Stocken Tomkins*; 20 bottom *Simon Brown*; 21 top left, bottom left and bottom right *Nicola Stocken Tomkins*; 21 top right *Simon Brown*; 22-23 *Cheryl Koralick*; 26-27 *Ebury Press/Dave King*; 28-29 *James Merrell*; 30 top left *Don Freeman*; 30 bottom right *Guy Hervais*; 31 *Andreas von Einsiedel*; 32-33 *Ebury Press/Dave King*; 34 *James Merrell*; 35 top left *James Merrell*; 35 bottom right *Simon Brown*; 36 top left *Simon Dodd*; 37 top right and bottom left *James Merrell*; 37 bottom right *Andreas von Einsiedel*; 38-39 *Ebury Press/Dave King*; 40 top left *James Merrell*; 41-42 *James Merrell*; 43 bottom right *Andreas von Einsiedel*; 44-45 *Ebury Press/Dave King*; 47 top left *James Mitchell*; 47 and bottom right *James Merrell*; 48 *Simon Dodd*; 50-51 *Ebury Press/Dave King*; 60-61 *Andreas von Einsiedel*; 63 top right *Andreas von Einsiedel*; 66 bottom *Andreas von Einsiedel*; 71 bottom right *Andreas von Einsiedel*; 72 bottom right *Andreas von Einsiedel*; 74-83 *Anton Dijkgraaf*; 84 top left *Guy Hervais*; 84 top right and bottom right *Andreas von Einsiedel*; 85 *Guy Hervais*; 87 *Andreas von Einsiedel*; 89 *Guy Hervais*; 90-91 *Journal de la Maison/Gilles Trillard*; 92 top *Living/Otto Polman/Mirjam Bleeker*; 92 bottom *Journal de la Maison/Gilles Trillard*; 93-95 *Living/Otto Polman/Mirjam Bleeker*; 108 *Turgut Salgar*; 109 bottom right *Robert Harding Picture Library/James Strachan*; 110-113 *Turgut Salgar*; 114 *James Merrell*; 124-131 *David Bailey*; 132-137 *James Merrell*; 148-152 *English Heritage Photo Library/Jonathan Bailey*; 153-157 *Country Life Picture Library*; 158-159 *Arena/Alex Cayley*.

Every effort has been made to contact copyright holders. The Publishers will be pleased to make good in future editions or reprints any omissions or corrections brought to their attention.